Books by Brad Leithauser

P O E M S

N O V E L S

THE MAIL FROM
ANYWHERE

THE MAIL FROM ANYWHERE

P O E M S   B Y

BRAD LEITHAUSER

ALFRED A. KNOPF   NEW YORK   1990

AUTHOR'S NOTE

I take this chance to offer acknowledgments of two sorts. Most of these poems first appeared in magazines: "The Mail from Anywhere," "Rain & Snow," "Reykjavik Winter Couplets," "Through Two Windows," and "A Worded Welcome" in *The New Yorker;* "A Bowl of Chinese Fireworks," "A Candle," "Peninsular," and "A Night Dive" in *The London Review of Books;* "Old Bachelor Brother" and "Your Natural History" in *The Atlantic Monthly;* "North of Night" and the second section of "Two Grotesques" in *The New Republic;* "The Caller" and "Uncle Grant" in *The New Criterion;* "Signalled" in *The New York Review of Books;* "Plexal" in *Oxford Poetry;* "First Birthday" in *Poetry;* and "Glow" in *The American Scholar.* I thank the poetry editors of these publications; their acceptances have brought me much encouragement.

Encouragement has come as well out of a blue sky—or a sky-blue envelope. I thank the friends who have kept in touch with me during my travels in recent years. "Peninsular" is dedicated to Hargurchet Bhabra, "The Mail from Anywhere" to Kim and Marty Townsend, "Rain & Snow" to Yosuke Ejima, "A Bowl of Chinese Fireworks" to Jon Stallworthy, "A Worded Welcome" to Mark O'Donnell, "Reykjavik Winter Couplets" to Elizabeth Horne, "Two Grotesques" to Ann Alexandra Huse, "Plexal" to Howell Chickering, and "North of Night" to Jacky Simms. "Your Natural History" and "First Birthday" are for my wife, Mary Jo, and for my daughters, Emily and Hilary.

Library of Congress Cataloging-in-Publication Data

   Leithauser, Brad.
      The mail from anywhere : poems / Brad Leithauser. — 1st ed.
      p. cm.
      ISBN 0-394-58586-0
      I. Title.
      PS3562.E4623M3   1990
      811'.54—dc20   90-52954
                                          CIP

Manufactured in the United States of America

FOR ANN CLOSE

godmother
to
one of my children
and
all of my books

CONTENTS

I THE MAIL FROM ANYWHERE

I I YOU AND THEM

I I I A PEOPLED WORLD

I THE MAIL FROM ANYWHERE

TWO GROTESQUES

Could you ever have as much light as nature, as much heat as the sun?
And you speak of exaggeration, but how could you exaggerate when you
always fall short of nature?   Paul Gauguin

I. Sub-tropical

Evil's rife
out among the deep-
stacked prisms beyond the reef
where slip
those edgeless creatures grown
vast for the removal
of a man's leg from thrashing foot to
long-boned thigh in one
simple, sole-purposed, and sun-
shattering ascent.

Evil drifts
in cloud-packs at dawn
and on wet mountain down-drafts
as one
by one the feathers shriek
with icy laughter
and the webs shiver into view—dense,
fine as a sawfly's
coigned, multiplicated eyes,
lifted, face to face.

The flies must
serve the sun as fuel,
as too the stars, the torn mist,
and all
the readied sky tumble
inward to make room
for that blazing which demands quite this
massive an outlay
to see its flames fed each day,
but which will be fed.

Evil goes
through the leafy snap
of the lizard's tongue, whose gaze
takes up
only the lights and darks
of food and peril,
filtering through the volcanic blooms—
red, gold, red—to where
masked beetles gather round their
furred, subsident throne.

In the hills,
under fronds ribbed for
bearing home a boar, are holes
that stare
into a starless black,
where in depths beyond
thinking one scream pursues another
over bladed stones,
over coral, over bones
preserved in salt. E-

vil—and what
word else to explain
that stealth as the mosses wait
to skin
their victims? Or why those
voluble monkeys,
quick with fever, have learned to fly so
high with their burning
leapings? Or that that's turning
counterclockwise in

the live, vile
muckwork of the swamp,
conceptioned under a veil
of plump,
blood-metabolizing
gnats? . . . Straitened as his
years, the space a man was meant for, some
tipped rows—breadfruit, bean—
wrested from the drowning green
and blue, hill and sea.

Brief, the sun's
warmth underfoot at
dusk—solace, and warning, since
you'd best
hold to that sole-warming sun
when the moon rises
to whisper the evil leaves awake•
and, treacherously,
to blaze fresh paths on the sea,
where no man can walk.

II. Sub-arctic

Smoke echoes up from a deep fault.
Clearly the hills are bottomed on
    A recessed lake of fire.
The stiffening winds blow and blow without a halt.
A day, a week goes by, and not one bird goes by.
    Perhaps the glacier's mounting toward
        The unclaimed sky.

In the first real darks of autumn the
    tundral winds into the hill-caves come
        tumbling, dry like the whispered snapping,
            amplified a millionfold, of a leaping
                candle . . . Only the warmth is missing.

In winter when the light retreats
No dawn with its enfeebled clouds
    And flat, off-center sun
Can bring it back. That's done at midnight, when the sheets
Of black-born blues and yellows waver and take flight,
Throwing across the stars a cover
    Like candlelight.

(That would be it, the one, the uni-
versal flame—our unreal,
sidereal taper, asway to drafty
transpirations huge beyond any
conceiving. Only the warmth is missing.)

Wrapped each in ice, the bodies go
Bump-bumping downriver in spring
From the high, cracking hills
Where the encasing's done. For all their numbers, though,
The current-clogging multitudes, there's not a trace
Of any body once the melting's
Taken place.

Meanwhile, a summer sun pours itself into a
small blue pool that, equal to anything,
catches it all without rising—merely one
feat in a land of miracles where only
the living and the dead are missing.

THE MAIL FROM ANYWHERE

Mail from pretty much anywhere was nearly
A month in crossing the seas and climbing that island's
Burning hillside. Each day, the heat rose early
And the noon hours called only for a can
Of beer, a cot, and the expunging silence
      Of an electric fan.

The ocean was a blue the sun brought forcibly
To whiteness and the hills a blackened green
Forced white as well. At first you couldn't see
A thing when you groped your way indoors, but soon
Out of the darkness it tumbled, the old scene—
      Chest, table, folding lawn

Chair, hanging calendar, pint-size fridge, sink—
And every stray detail seen to and pieced
Together, including even that runaway blink
Of iridescent green on the backs of the brown
Lizards that prowled the walls. (They were supposed
      To keep the insects down.)

Sunsets were jarring, uncontrolled events,
The monstrously expansive greenery
Revealed at last as veined with blood. But once
The sun was gone, sometimes, a sourceless flush
Would follow, like no other, and the sea,
      Internally awash

With light, turn weightless, while down the beach a masked
Figure might trudge ashore from out a cloud . . .
The air would cool, grow warmly rich with massed
Exploratory scents, and the thoroughfare
Of the Milky Way unroll like an open road,
      As happens only where

All cities lie well under the horizon,
And on such evenings, when the wind was flat,
The bay unruffled, and no moon yet risen,
The heavens would double—stars above, below . . .
That those glints were but the ghosts of fires lit
      Millennia ago,

Such being the time light takes to traverse the sky,
Seems an almost too familiar notion, not
To be doubted—and not to be believed. For try
As we may, and must, the numbers our minds uncover
Will never fit inside our heads. And yet,
      When morning would deliver

Another sort of light—that of a sky-
Blue envelope—here was a gap that could
Be taken in and understood:
              to know,
As the heat-loosened glue gave easily
To your blunt fingers, *A few weeks ago,*
    Someone was thinking of me.

RAIN & SNOW

I

When, with a shiver, after
weeks of such dryness, the rain
comes, it comes as in answer
to yearnings not bound within
the twin, tight kingdoms of plants
and animals—as if those
loose, nerveless others (the fence
pales and roof pantiles, the clothes-
lines and sighing, tire-stroked street),
that lodge here merely, bearing
no gift for flight, at least might
savor a sense of being,
on the outside, anyway,
as free-running as the sea.

11

II

Not simply unforeseen . . . but
unforeseeable: just so
are these angling oddments cut
from a black, unyielding sky.
Yet it seems the stooping hills
have been waiting to lighten;
and waiting the housetop tiles,
for a film through which to burn,
under-brightly; and waiting—
having first swallowed every
city glimmer in passing—
the river, waiting to be
visibly undazzled by
even beauty so unlikely.

Daybreaks to those gray
Voices pushing out
The dark's darker
Voices. And the way

Adoze at times in Kyoto
To the nudgings of a neighbor's
Television and the set
Picking up the radio

My parents always woke to
Morning passing through
Morning on
The other side

Of the wall
Of the world
So early. All
Of those voices

Pushing back
The night as they must
Black into black
The news going on

Out
As it ought
And in coming in
By way of those thin

Pulsed voices saying
On most days Yes it's all right
Everything held together
Through the night

The world is just
Where you left it
Out there you must
Go out in it. Increasingly

The news
Doesn't it
Comes like this
Bodiless

And over blue
Curved reaches the voices clearer
Though farther
Linking us to

Our leaders and voter
Profiles gain
And loss the roaming walls
Of local storms our falling rain

Forests the murmur
Of distant hunger
The murder
Of some public

Dignitary
One of ours and yet
The name not
Caught.

The dead
Pyramid largely
Under us and in their mounting
Numbers would rise

Airing complaints
Apologies second
Thoughts saying Still
Uncorrected

The old mistake
But we're sorry
To wake you we're
Sorry and you must wake.

NORTH OF NIGHT

(ON THE SUMMER SOLSTICE)

To a mind uprooted from
a shaking hour's all but upright nap
   it made sense
to view our poleward journey not
as the enactment of any human plan
but something conceived and piloted
   solely by the plane—

   as though *it* realized that,
this time of year, the way to pursue any
   sun gone west
was not by going west; no—north . . . Maine, Nova
Scotia, Labrador, and that in time our flight
would open, over Greenland, on groundless concourses
   where the wings would float

   through light undimmed by dusk, high
over snowy cloudbanks, higher still over shelved
   hills of snow.
Day everlasting: north of night: and to see in this
a place where metal was meant to find voice
(as anvils ring to their mallets, the sawn tin
   whistles in its vise,

nails call *out* when clasped within
a hammer's claw) and where rare flocks of us
     (metal birds,
homing birds) were destined to gather, and we
but the earliest arrivals to an immense,
wheeling, gleam-relaying rendezvous—
     even that made sense.

The sheerly steadied stubborn tons of it

    when you close your eyes
    are something massed
    as a good, pleasing
pressure inside your chest.

The overlapping spill and sinkage of it

    like a wet breeze
    under the wet stars
    works through the dark
revolvings of your ears.

Blindly, you feel it, out there, know you are

    up beside
    an immensity
    that coolly turns
the August sun away.

Or open wide your eyes—they open on

    the mine-black walls
    of the glacier's end,
    hard-fitted with the stones
of its raw erosions. To stand

before what nightless summer cannot melt

    and winter will
    do nothing but
    enlarge upon
surprisingly is not

for you an opportunity so much

    to marvel as,
    with time, to ponder
    how so centerless a coldness
dwindles one's gift for wonder.

Before the outward-locking expulsiveness

    of it, the sharpened
    denial of it,
    you might find helpful
a colossal but simple conceit:

the glacier is a ship; the stones,

    its single freight;
    the sea, its port.
    Home, homeward bound . . .
and casting off from a height

that makes a small, whimsical joke

of whatever gesture—
call or signal—
you'd care to offer
by way of a farewell.

According to
your point of view,
it stands for love—
or hell posed starkly.
I'm thinking of
the single fellow
who hunches darkly,
as though with shame,
there at the blue-yellow
center of the flame.

REYKJAVIK WINTER COUPLETS

I

One senses
Waking at dark
The promise of dark
For hours yet. The same
Two feet of snow and laval
Outcroppings and a car turning over
Over in search of the position where
The hum of a dream commences.

II

Disorder's
Undone a few feet
From the bakery door
Where snow-blasting winds
Run up against the firm smell
Of bread baking—loaves white as snow
Within, and shovelled like snow, soon, from
The oven's blackened borders.

III

The thrashing
And the dead, dumped
From nets to baskets,
Like stolen goods under the old
Warehouse's one bulb gleam. Frantic,
Nearing, the search for them continues:
Hear the wind at the door and the sea, leaving
   No stone unturned, crashing.

IV

As sequel
To a nightcap
Cup of cocoa comes
(Sleep, too, coming on)
The middleman's floating knowledge
That the clouds of steam drifting up
And, out there, the clouds of snow coming down
   Are perfectly equal.

THROUGH TWO WINDOWS

Comforting, in its way, how, wherever you may be,
the effect's so much the same—walking in Rome,

say, or Reykjavik, or one of those rust-red
Missouri rivertowns where we all were born and grew,

you merely glance right up into somebody's home,
catching the sky, out back, through two

sets of windows, and are in a sense home free:
free of everywhere you've lived, everything you've read.

It's a tinted sky—as if by the lives bound like a book
between its panes—and so not quite the one

you're standing under. No wonder, then, these odd un-
sorted feelings of exclusion and remorse . . .

all a small price to pay for any look
at the roof of another world, of course.

Late
afternoon light,
and such
a pretty touch—
the way the sun, slow-
wheeling down the wall
in a fall of white on white,
clear into gold explodes
just upon reaching the bowl
of elaborate, illicit fireworks
reserved for this evening's party.

Not
until the night
has grown
into its own
at last, drinks downed,
dinner in all its courses done,
and the guests, trailing bright
inquisitive laughter, led
out onto the black lawn,
will the show start, but already now,
at the sun's touch, it's as if a new

                    phase
            has come, a fuse
                begun
            to sizzle. One
    by one, the sun picks out
        the big bowl's contents: a long-
    tailed dragon first, from whose
    gaping leer a leaping tongue
        of particolored flame's to spring;
    next, a paisley-papered Roman
    candle; then a sort of bouquet,

                    bound
            by rubber band,
                of blue-
            and-yellow two-
    stage rockets, and a yacht, whose
        maiden voyage (tonight, in a hose-
    filled pail) will raise a grand
    canopy of stars from the slim pole of its
        smokestack. If, just now, a trace
    of pink, of perishable rose, robs some
    burnish from the day, as if to say,

Soon
this sun-set scene
must shift,
its glories drift
off elsewhere—in the meanwhile,
anyway, our dragon sits in style
atop a glowing treasure-stack,
and with the cool, expansive self-
possession of his kind,
grins extravagantly back
at the blaze that enriches him.

I I. YOU AND THEM

Below, on the badly cracked floor
of their heated den, distanced from you by a great
sheet of glass, the pythons (four,
maybe five in all—hard to say for all

the tricky intricacies of their self-made knot)
are sleeping. Though indiscriminately
accommodating (head sunk dreamily in the slot
of another's upflung ribcage, conforming tail warming

still another's tail), they ask to be
counted one by one, tapered end
to end methodically—
a task to which the eye turns

happily, stroking down in gratified leisure
over the charm-inlaid, the bright brute primitive
glamour of their skins. The scales, the larger
of them, anyway, are big as coins,

and metallic, too, in the severe,
exclusionary span of their burnished, brown-
centered spectrum; these creatures come as near
as blooded beings can to seeming

offspring of a blacksmith's lair,
linkages fused under hammers and a bitter sudden
searing kiss of steam.
                              When, where—
all unclear, how the shift begins, but now it's

31

certain everything's already
moving or must at once be moving; once the long
unclustering's begun, there's not a body
to the whole collective coil

can remain quite as it was: for each,
new, individuating torsions to
work out, new blind ends to reach
within a parted mesh of flexings and dry

oozings. Unclear, as well,
what solidifying hunger or stiffness
pin-prompted the groundswell,
but plainly the correspondences in this den

remain unexpectedly tight—
as with some pared mathematics
wherein the modification, however slight,
of a single postulate inevitably

everts a balance elsewhere, or some ideal
body politic for whom the emergent grievance
of a lone member means the commonweal
itself wants amendment.
                                        Their settling down,

their easeful inching toward one several slumber,
arrives in progressive laxings—
attended, diminishingly, by a number
of afterthought-like adjustments

to show that while at last they've shaped
some workable emplacement, in which to rest
inclusively, they've escaped again
the unwaking repose of perfection.

Impulse alone, indicating
　　what might be called
　a byway off a detour's detour,
led me suddenly to stop the car,
　　rented in Reykjavik a week before,

　　zip my parka tight to the chin,
　　　and, bare hands balled
　　in its pockets, strike off
briskly, as though by plan, toward a rough-
　angled, distant shoreline. Now if

　　one were assembling, as I guess I was,
　　　some sort of file
　　entitled Uninviting Vistas,
here was one—grayly colorless,
　　hugely creatureless—demanding pride of place:

　　a laval sea of stone extending
　　　mile upon mile,
　　and all of it still brokenly
flowing, in lichen-whitecapped waves, toward a gray,
　　cold, contrarily breaking sea.

　　To their frozen opposition I'd brought
　　　a freezing one,
　　leaning hard against the shrill
resistance of a wind that, at the arrival
　　of a figure at once vertical

and mobile, seemed ferociously
    to stiffen. None
of my trudging worked to bring
the sea any nearer. My cheeks stung
    for a little while, before going

    deeply numb . . . Impulse, and an eye out
        for any kind
    of change, began to reconnoiter,
seizing upon a low rise some ways over
        on the left: I took another

        detour, hand-scrambled up
            the slope to find
        a sort of crater below, in which some
ferns and short grasses stood—as well as a grim-
    eyed, wide-shouldered, skewbald ram.

        Clearly, he didn't like my looks . . .
            and I should add
        (laughable, but only in retrospect)
I was unhinged a bit by those cruelly hooked
    horns of his. Well, we locked

        glances, for one long moment; it seems
            that each had had
        enough of being buffeted and wasn't
about to forfeit the barest shelter without
    a mental fight. Edginess did ease somewhat

when I dropped to a crouch, although
remaining far
from easy; but if he did, eventually, resume
his grazing, it took still more time
for me to adjust to *him,*

having first to unload my sense of
something bizarre
or noble or at least meaningful
in his having chosen to make his meal
in such an embittered locale.

Blind distrust needed additional
moments to close
upon the simple lesson in the air—
no place is out-of-the-way to the creature
grounding its livelihood there—

a message of concern
only to those
so rootless somehow they might
even for a moment have forgotten it.

Given a day
that opened in a brilliant show
of sea-washed sun,
one might naturally have predicted—
this being Reykjavik—that we'd have snow
before the day was done;
snow, anyway,

is what we get,
with winds whipped to a low-grade squall
and a bay drowned
in whitecaps. Shoulders up, chin lowered,
hands pocketed, I'm shuffling fast, like all
those few who haven't found
their shelter yet,

when something queer
in a window across the street,
a gold-green glow,
lights like a signal and I stop,
turn, look, squint, lose it in another sheet
of snow . . . And that's all—though
it would appear

the thing demands
a closer look, but who's to know?
 I hesitate,
weighing an urge for puzzle-solving
against the weather, then decide I'll go
 over to investigate . . .
 The window stands

 just a few feet
from the slush-piled sidewalk, and near
 enough to study
the cacti forest on the sill
in all its intricate, delicate, clear-
cut beauty. Now anybody
 who'd crossed the street

 on such a day,
summoned by some *What could that be?*,
 would likely feel
near-duty-bound to look these over;
but duty's not, in fact, required of me—
 the vision they reveal
 (basking away

beneath the sun
of an unseen ceiling spotlight,
    its prising touch
unearthing greens whose deepness hints
at some remote and all but weathertight
felicity) is such
    a striking one.

*   *   *

As the snowflakes
shiver and rap against the glass,
    the eye delights
in going where the hand could not—
spiraling down a needle-strung crevasse,
it halts, adjusts its sights,
    and lightly makes

a little jump,
negotiates a passage through
    dense battle lines
of live barbed wire, then takes another
leap, and, a tranquil end sprung into view,
ascends a spine of spines,
    up to the plump,

39

towering tip,
whose fine-toothed, clockwork blossom may,
with time, unwind
itself. For all their independent
rigor, the cacti seem to share a way
of life, a breadth, a kind
of fellowship . . .

                ★   ★   ★

Enough — the rain
of snow pools on the windowsill.
It's late. The street
grows dark. Time to be off, although
there's time for one more mental snapshot (still
hoping to freeze their heat
upon the brain);

and time enough,
as well, for noticing how rich,
    tier upon tier,
are the resources the mind brings
to even its littlest joys, like this, in which
a worldly inner ear
thrills to a rough-

tongued wonder as
a breathless inner voice exclaims,
How strong they look!

It's an early fall, perhaps,
Or a late flight. Whatever—here's
A hotfooting robin, not yet gone
South, and out to forage,
From a gilded lawn
Whose leaf-carpet appears
To turn his breast near-brown,
A few last-minute scraps.

Come March, though,
To these same eyes (and this same
Lawn, its threadbare snow
Rolled up and put in storage),
How much brighter's grown the glow
Thrown by that small brown flame!

A NIGHT DIVE

It feels so much
Like waking, this
Rising after
Forty minutes
Under forty
Feet of water;
And to fill your
Life-vest, breath by
Breath, while floating
Nearer a moon
Mounted just high
Enough to have
Lost all trace of
Gold and have turned
A cool silver
Is seemingly
To come at once
Greatly before
The drawing source
Of every blood-
 Tide sleeplessness.

For where, unless
In sleep, have you
Done this before—
Climbing, a lamp
Strapped to your wrist,
Up from the paired
Embers of dim
Crustaceal lives
Fast in polyp-
Padded pockets
At the bottom,
From moray eels,
So much like slow
Flying snakes, from
Schools in flurried
Scatterings and
Voluminous
Fans tenderly
Engorging what
Squiggling minims
   The current brings?

To rise, through rings
On widening
Rings of coded
Compartments-in-
Flux, up to glimpse
Just overhead
The surface where
A kit of bones
Goes dancing like
A skeleton
On a mirror,
And with a crash
To shatter it,
To throw the sea
Clear off your head,
And find the boat
Where it should be,
Nearby and yet
Not yet so near
One cannot feel
Oneself alone

(Alone within
A sort of field
Where the moon takes
The shivered path
Of a paving
Older by far
Than anything
Pick and shovel
Ever aired) is
To confront, and
As though at last,
The stripped, whited
Ruin written
Into every
Sketchy neural
Blueprint . . . and yet
To confront it
With a moving
Tranquillity,
A long inkling
That one's fears, too,

Are trifling. *You*
Will come purely
To nothing is
Of course its pain-
Fully unmixed
Message, but who,
Adrift, head moon-
Touched here, could fly
The illusion
That it's enough
Merely to be
A warm, blooded
Body within
So vast a sea? —
Or that other,
By which even
Ever-lightless
Depths are richer
For having some
Mobile mind free-
Floating upon them?

I I I.   A PEOPLED WORLD

Afloat within
an empty sea, and seemingly at home
up there, and floating, too, down here, inside the twin
circles of my binoculars, he ventures quite
without support, since the lifelines
that bond him to that bright
expansive dome

above his head
remain, no matter how I squint and strain,
invisible. Just so: a man's deposited
upon a throne of air, and while he finds it ample,
finds, too, it will not hold him—just.
The resolution's simple:
he must come down,

then. Down through stacked
transparencies, the inward march of far
horizons, he drops—valleys, hills, and meadows cracked
by stationary streams, farms, fences, dots of wool
like waiting building blocks of cloud . . .
No more removable
than the days are

that separate
yearning from some long-planned red-letter day
is each of the one-metre rungs upon that great
notional ladder which attaches him to us;
    each outlays its own vista; each is
        a sort of terminus
            along the way.

    Rate, route are set—
the vectored clash of wind and gravitation
fixes the exact details of his arrival. Yet,
from where he loosely stands, views breathlessly would quicken:
    blurred trees come crisply into leaf,
        a lazing stream awaken
            lightly, to motion

        throughout a place
    whose every glancing form grows sharper-edged—
detail within detail until, with an embrace
whose ardor pops the massive thought-balloon above
    his little head, he meets, as pledged,
        the rich, soiled earnest of
            a peopled world.

Harmless, no doubt,
Because hopeless, no doubt, yet far
From hurtless, this nightly not
Being where you are—
Where, somewhere, you go right on being
That miraculously out-
Fitted and not quite conceivably
Tactile matter of yourself. Seeing
How this having you constantly not here
Appears to be my vacant lot
In life, why so implausible, then—that with the mere
Business of breathing, the body's slow
Expulsion of what has turned out to be
        Useless, you'd truly disappear? But no—

        No means, no hope
Of shaking you, though you're not here.
Days, days on end, no end, and so fully aware that I'm
Aware of just how perfectly absurd
It is—how, ever, you pull on me, as though
A magnet to every tiny-toothed gear
And staple, brad and screw, all the drill-
Bits and fishhooks, the hammer claws
And awls, and the metal rope,
Wrenches, vises, planes, rasps, and circular saws
In my belly . . . When, some nights ago, I heard
A summons that withdrew during my climb
Toward wakefulness, until
        I knew it was come from no

Physical phone,
But some dream hook-up, I can't explain just
How desolating that was—only ask you to think
Of a phone ringing to wake the dead in some low-
Ceilinged office whose shades are drawn,
Some Bureau of Incorporations, Inc.,
Some annex of your local Heartfelt Loan,
Ltd., long hours after everyone's gone
Home. No doubt it's some mistake and our
Caller hasn't a prayer of bringing
Anyone to the receiver at this hour,
But still it goes on, that shaded ringing . . .
Still it all goes on, and still, my dear, I must
        Say that I can't say you've brought no

        Pleasure to me—
Pleased, anyhow, at having you enrich
My sense of worlds surrounding ours, in which
(Wouldn't you know?) we are invariably
Lovers. Still, *still no good* . . . No good, you see,
Unless you see, and I don't think you do,
How, daily, you're so painfully untrue
To all those worlds, and what a weight for me
It is, night after night, to field the same
Fatiguingly fresh, petulant demands
For entrance to that room—really not so far—
Where you and I a little shyly are
Undressing and you, yes, whisper my name,
        And I take your head in my hands.

YOUR NATURAL HISTORY

The night of your conception, from the floor
Where we were lying and your mother now
Lay sleeping, I arose. I locked the door,
Lingering there a minute to watch how
The firelight fanned her face and throat, then went
On tiptoe to the misted window, cleared
A space, and found, high over the snow-bent
Forest, a dwindled moon, whose edges bleared
At my slowed breathing—it was all as frail
As that—while far away, or in my mind
Alone perhaps, a dog sent up a wail
That showed him for a wolf. Your mother whined,
As with a dream; a log collapsed; and then
I fingerprinted FIRE upon the pane.

Dawn, and white lungs, and since it was my turn
To start the fire, I was the first from bed.
Downstairs, where we'd lain watching the logs burn
Gold, red, red to a gray whose core was red,
A killing cold was sliding down the flue.
Yet there it was, cool as the hand of fate:
My FIRE, preserved in hoar-frost, and I knew
She'd love this too.
                              Well . . . let the (other) fire wait?
Or wake her now? Or—as seemed kindest—make
Of this the day's first story, one that I
Might serve with coffee, last night's apple cake,
And a thawed room? I piled the fireplace high,
And struck a match, wresting a flame, your flame,
From ice. By just such miracles you came.

FIRST BIRTHDAY

You have your one word, which fills you to brimming.
It's what's first to be done on waking,
Often the last at day-dimming:
Lunge out an arm fiercely,
As though your heart were breaking,
Stab a finger at some stray illumination—
Lamp, mirror, distant dinner candle—
And make your piercing identification,

"'ight! 'ight! 'ight!"
Littlest digit, you've got the world by the handle.
Things must open for you, you take on height,
Your sole sound in time reveal itself
As might, too, and flight. And fright.
Some will be gone. But you will come right.

The jet-lagged, dragged-out series of events
That brought me here—to a ramshackle
And very cheap hotel
On the outskirts of an immense
Asian city, with a view
Of a bare-bones army of aerials
Pitched on the rain-strafed pantiles
Of rank on rank of roofs sagged out of true,
Jalopies rusting on the puddled street,
A mystery shop whose charactered awning
Day after day gives up no meaning,
A straitened bar where workmen, on their feet,
Throw down their beer and whiskeys while
A wet, rat-witted dog digs up a meal—

Is in the past. What matters now
Is just that you, almost precisely,
Are half a world away. And an uneasy
Sense of this distance as somehow
Unbridgeable, as though no flight,
However long, those big parental engines
Shouldering on across the falling time zones,
Could ever reunite
The two of us, matters as well.
It's like a rip in some
Canvas whose scene must also show the seam
Forever—or one of those core
Tectonic rifts, blooded with fire, that will
Never arrange itself entire once more.

—Fanciful, is it, to see
Our separation on so grand a scale?
For idle weeks on end I ransacked my skull,
Seeking the name of that appealingly
Symbolic, numbingly gigantic mass
Which, once, held all our continents within
A single shore. But chain on chain,
And age through age, the hills set out across
The sea—seemingly driven to the task
Of figuring themselves into the shape
Our maps have made our own; it was so queer,
This sense of having no books here
In which to look it up,
And no one to ask.

Seen close enough, events are seen to have
No causes. Just say, then, it's been my luck,
Or lot, to spend the last few months in Bangkok—
Hot little room whose windows give
Out on this city which everybody knows
Has grown too big, and keeps on growing, since
We cannot stop growing. It's most intense
Late in the day—the heat, the noise,
Everything coming, step by step,
To an unbreathable, furious standstill,
And from every automobile,
It seems, the familiar, futile
Pounded-out chorus of horns taken up:
We cannot stop, we cannot stop.

And then it came to me,
The name—Pangea—just as I'd stepped out
A bakery door, a long, unwrapped baguette
Under my sweat-damp arm. Initially,
I didn't grasp (didn't, in fact, until
Today) why the name surfaced when it did:
An echo of the French for *bread.*
Or maybe not? The mind is fanciful . . .
In any case, I liked this notion
Of old vocabularies waiting there,
Somewhere, still in the head—within, afar—
As if those languages that would appear
Lost with the rest of one's schooling are
Continuously in motion,

And now and then, though barely heard,
Make some restorative connection,
Issue some happy call to action:
Give us this day our daily word.
And would you take me at my word
If I confessed it thrilled me, *thrilled* me, yes—
This inkling of some temporary egress
From that flat dread that says that if one could
Shut out the whole world's clamor.
For just a moment, one would encounter then
Not peace but—faintly, fatefully instead—
A rap-rap-rapping like a distant hammer:
Doors going shut, minutely, one
By one by one inside one's head.

I'd rather think that any such
Lifelong diminution will
Be met by compensations, that the whole
Process be one of fair exchange, by which
What's paid out in the going from
Conception to demise, points C and D,
Between which life's the shortest path, will be
Repaid—as will the losses tedium
Inflicts and all of those conceived in fear,
As when a sort of curtain slides
Away and in stunned irreality
The whole span of one's life comes clear
In all its stripped, bare-bones simplicity—
The clearer for the darkness on both sides.

I picture you (and would you picture me?
Please—beginning with a room
Kept, as if to make some claim
Or point, immaculate. And, pointedly
Again, note that it offers none of your
Pensive expatriate's standard props—
No smokes, no drinks. A can of beer, perhaps,
At dusk but—certainly—none of those snow-pure
Powders, so cheap out here, that cross the seas,
Somehow, to reach the streets of home. I'm trim,
Neat, shaved. I have not found my calling,
True, but that isn't why I came.
My eyes are wide, and I'd like to think at ease,
Watching the street. It's nightfall. Rain is falling.)

I picture you seated . . . You're sitting by
A silvered window, since I'd have it rain
There as well, where it is dawn
Not dusk, a world from here. You're wondering why
Everything—everything—turns out the way
It does. You share my sense of just how deeply
Generous is the rain, and how completely
Undeserved its gift—and, in the final say,
How fruitless. You would see things straight . . .
Oh, you'd escape from time, and all of that,
Even as you, too, realize
What's likely to be windowed from that room
Wherein no seconds tick, no hours boom,
Is the world breaking up before one's eyes.

It was the trip up the Amazon
At the age of twelve that, or so
The boy's mother later insisted,
Undid his wits. How had she ever
Agreed to such a plan? She *had* resisted,
Of course, but the boy's rootless Uncle John,
Writing from a museum faraway
In Washington, and the hell-bent child
Himself, had, between them, won the day
Somehow and made her do what never
She should have done: she let the boy go.
No wonder, what with months in the wild—
Savages, the jungle, food, heat, rain—
He'd caught some fever of the brain.

Whatever the case, this boy, my great-
Uncle Grant, came home to Tennessee
And never left the farm again
For long. Deaths, heat, harvests, he stayed on,
Fished the local Amazon,
Hunted the circling hills. The farm passed
To Alfred, his older brother,
Whose consumptive wife, just twenty-three
And pregnant with her third, miscarried
Ten days before spitting up her last
Life-blood. After a frantic month's wait,
Alfred found his children a new mother—
And, in all, he made his brother ten
Times an uncle. Grant never married.

. . . But the story's more complicated
Than this, since Grant doggedly pursued
An alternate livelihood throughout
His life. At sixteen he sent a kind
Of mash note to his mentor,
Alexander Graham Bell, whose
Avuncular, long, and long-awaited
Reply (from Nova Scotia!) closed — "Choose
Your goals with care, large and small.
Question everything, but never doubt
The resource of the human mind,
My boy." Perhaps it was this call
From Bell, and not the jungle, that skewed
Grant's wits: he became an inventor.

Which was — or was if one can tell
By results alone — the purest folly. His
Dream was of a kind of workbench El
Dorado, where the gold of free
Fancy, mined systematically
At last, would sift itself out.
Not a thing came of his labors
In the end, excepting some
Dubious family tales and — no doubt —
Much laughter for and from the neighbors.
But in the long view — as, say, from
The windows of a plane — bit
By bit his failures feed a soil that is
The richer for those who resisted it . . .

We arrived—my brother and I, each
Competingly agog with the wonder
That boyhood takes in flight—
At the Nashville Airport, there
Met by our tall Aunt Elaine, under
Whose not always watchful eye
We'd spend a month. Next day, we were met by
A list of chores, including some manure
In need of a shovel, which, to be sure,
Was a useful task—if meant to teach
Two city boys never to make light
Of earthbound employment.
                                            Everywhere
Her farm called us with places to explore,
But it wasn't many days before

We'd turned the lock on that old door
And clambered up some stairs to what
Still was called Grant's Laboratory.
It was a low, narrow room, a sort
Of loft above a sort of shed.
Surprisingly, a number of tools
And things still lay outspread
On the cobwebbed table—pulleys, rope, spools
Of wire, bottled powders, a score
Of nuts and bolts, a cracked retort—
The leavings of a mind caught
Up in the perpetual motion
Of the alchemist's lead-fueled notion
Of a lasting conversion to glory.

This was late afternoon. The sun
Again had turned to gold. The room's one
Window gave upon some lilac bushes
On which a dreamer's eye might fall
In those whiled hours when it seems
Unclear if he but dreams or starts to feel
The first buried birth-pushes
Of something real
And richly practical. If Grant's dreams
Were dreams, he breathed no final discontent
In his will, wherein he grandly granted "all
Fruits of my scientific industry,
Now, and in perpetuity,
To the United States Government."

THE CALLER

After the final and all-
But-unnecessary bell, most everyone
Already gone, might come a few last wheeling
Cries, goodbyes, sometimes a brief
Stab of laughter, the last light sliding
Footfalls of this year's children, or
The so much weightier, wider striding
Of one of her colleagues, sweeping the hall
Of its echoes, and then, wider yet, a feeling
Of feeling the building itself being done
For the day—as if it, too, waited for
This moment, and met it with relief.

So she would sit. The room was hers. Late
Afterschool sun climbed the legs
Of the pine desk turned out, years ago,
From the town's own mill. From here: a view
Of Stoner's Hardware, the billiard hall,
And past the tracks, and drearier
Still, the shacklike houses where the town dregs
Lived out their shackled lives, and lastly, below
The town, and also well above it all—
Gray as steel sometimes, sometimes a blue
Earth's freshest eye could but approximate—
The Lake, the only one, her Superior.

So she would sit, and smoke. Her reign here,
In this very room, was now closing upon
Three decades, but always she'd felt bound,
At least until this, her fifty-seventh year,
Never to light up inside it.
Before, she'd shut herself up in what
Was grandly called The Faculty Salon —
That dark and dreary hole. But
No more, no more attempting to hide it . . .
She'd watch the Lake and light up openly —
For anyone and everyone to see —
Had there been, at this hour, someone still around.

Once this same lake was sailed by a giant
Soul, Henry Longfellow, who drifted
On purest tides of inspiration —
This the shining Big-Sea-Water
Of the Arrow Maker's Daughter,
The belov'd of Hiawatha. Oh,
Poetry! On the walls it was Keats, Blake —
Both lamb and tiger — Lanier and Bryant,
And Longfellow over the window, so
The right imagination might be ever lifted
At having read, early on, lines and lake
Together. But where was that imagination?

So she would sit, doubting and smoking freely,
In this her fifty-seventh year. She knew she'd
Scared them all, from the children on up, really:
Parents, teachers—and that squirming sinner
Of a superintendent, too. And she didn't need
Her height to work this on them, though
As for that, proudly six feet tall she stood. No,
This was the fear that those that have no inner
Elevation always feel for those that do.
She knew her poetry. And by God she knew
There wasn't a soul in this sawdust town
Who could, when she felt rightful, stare her down.

(*What a scowl that woman had!* ... And by
Such phrases, a few thin anecdotes, and one brown
Photograph, this woman, Lucinda Stitt, came down
To me. That's her younger brother, my
Great-uncle Chuck beside her, his cane
The hook to a youthful mishap at the mill.
They lived together. He grins, but she—it's plain—
Distrusts the photographer, whose portrait, cracked
As it is, bears all her rightfulness intact.
She's in her prime, clearly, with some time still
Before cracks of another sort would appear—
In that, her fifty-seventh year.)

What queerish notions, at day's end, brooding
Brings to mind! Sitting, smoking, in a gray-
Golden cloud, she'd wind up recalling
A chant—the boys—so many years ago—and how
Angry it once made her—how angry even now!
. . . She would be newly burning at the way
They had gone on, the boys, including
That jug-eared Gus Gustafsson, bawling
Lucinda, Lucinda, she fell out of the winda.
This was for them the height of wit!
Poetry's paragon! She heard them, chanting it
Stupidly still: *Lucinda, Lucinda . . .*

What was the use of home at night,
His slap of fork and spoon, the lounging phlegm
In his throat, the clearing of that throat
To usher in the utterance of one more gem
Of wisdom? What earthly use? Better to float
Right here, on tides of smoke, still in sight
Of the Lake—gray as steel, blue as flame—
And turn on not one light, but let the room
Go gold, go gray, knowing that of course
He would come, for there was no force
Under heaven to keep him back, come on the same
Cane-clatter, to coax her down from the gloom.

(*Well, she was an odd one, that one, Brad,*
My grandpa once told me, with a curved
Nudge to the glance maybe meant to suggest,
Man-to-future-man, that she was one who'd had
No use for men. And yet, on a raw,
Rain-paned fall afternoon, Grandma imparted
A counter impression, when she observed,
What a man never seems to realize
Is that even the stoniest
Looking woman may be broken hearted,
And for the first and only time I saw
A sort of soupy look come into her eyes.)

In winter, ice worked its way outwards from
The shore, outreaching just as if, at last,
About to hazard an actual crossing,
But always followed days of accounting
When, loud as riflefire, it shattered to show
The bright blue burning down below.
No log burned blue as that tossing
Water burned . . . Whyever did it call her so
Fiercely, that blue out of blue, as if some
Answer were wanted she could not give it, no,
It wasn't inside her, no, as the days passed,
Summer coming on, the sun remounting

The legs of her desk, as she waited for the light
To fade, for the ever later dark to come,
For an escape from that man, her clown-
Like caller, looking for all the world like some
Laughably miscast swain in one of the absurd
Town theatricals, mooning out there
On the playground, school being locked up tight,
His round face trained on her upper
Row of windows, baying Come on down,
And scratching his ear, wondering if she'd heard,
Then baying, sweetly, Come down,
Come down, Lucinda, I've made you supper.

Dark would go the walls, rhyme on rhyme,
Now bringing unavoidably to mind
How these were nothing but words in the failing
Glow, one with the down-slipping dust-
Motes, streaks on the glass, red, threadbare
Carpet on the creaking bottom stair
Of home, some other home, and sooner, later,
The Lake must swallow them all, just
As it swallowed, now and then, a skater,
A sailor, whose bodies are flailing
All on the Lakefloor together, blind
As life, as light, as Time;

And colder than ice, somehow, that shattering
Water, and always him coming, clattering
His stick, calling Come down, as if some use
To that, but oh, let him wait, and wait for
The match to bite and the letting loose
Of another ghost of smoke, him calling at the winda,
The window, her name, that man, who won't go 'way,
Shattering the peace, your peace, calling Lucinda,
But he can wait for you, you needn't—no—
Answer, not until you've lit one more
Of the cigarettes that, with each passing day,
Prove harder to light your hands are shaking so.

OLD BACHELOR BROTHER

Here from his prominent but thankfully
uncentral position at the head of the church—
a flanking member of the groom's large party—
he stands and waits to watch the women march

up the wide aisle, just the way they did
at last night's long and leaden-joked rehearsal.
Only this time, it's all changed. There's now a crowd,
of course, and walls of lit stained glass, and Purcell

ringing from the rented organist,
and yet the major difference, the one
that hits his throat as a sort of smoky thirst,
is how, so far away, the church's main

doors are flung back, uncovering a square
of sun that streams into the narthex, so that
the women who materialize there
do so in blinding silhouette,

and these are not the women he has helloed
and kissed, and who have bored, ignored, or teased him,
but girls—whose high, garlanded hair goes haloed
by the noon-light . . . The years have dropped from them.

One by one they're bodied forth, edged with flame,
as new as flame, destined to part the sea
of faces on each side, and approaching him
in all their passionate anonymity.

A NOTE ABOUT THE AUTHOR

Brad Leithauser was born in Detroit, Michigan, in 1953. He graduated from Harvard College and Harvard Law School. He has been a Research Fellow at the Kyoto Comparative Law Center, Visiting Writer at Amherst College, and is currently a Lecturer at Mount Holyoke College. He was awarded a Fulbright Fellowship to teach at the University of Iceland in 1989, and recently joined the Editorial Board at the Book-of-the-Month Club. He lives with his wife, the poet Mary Jo Salter, and their two daughters, Emily and Hilary, in South Hadley, Massachusetts.

He is the author of two previous volumes of poetry, *Hundreds of Fireflies* (1982) and *Cats of the Temple* (1986), and two novels, *Equal Distance* (1985) and *Hence* (1989). His poems and critical articles have appeared in many places, among them *The New Yorker, The Atlantic Monthly, The New York Review of Books, Harper's, The New Republic,* and *The New Criterion.* He is the recipient of many awards for his writing, including a Guggenheim Fellowship, an Ingram Merrill grant, an Amy Lowell Poetry Travelling Scholarship, and a MacArthur Fellowship.

A NOTE ON THE TYPE

The text of this book was set in film in a typeface called Griffo, a camera version of Bembo, the well-known monotype face. The original cutting of Bembo was made by Francesco Griffo of Bologna only a few years after Columbus discovered America. It was named for Pietro Bembo, the celebrated Renaissance writer and humanist scholar who was made a cardinal and served as secretary to Pope Leo X. Sturdy, well-balanced, and finely proportioned, Bembo is a face of rare beauty. It is, at the same time, extremely legible in all of its sizes.

Composition by Superior Type, Champaign, Illinois

Printed and bound by Halliday Lithographers
West Hanover, Massachusetts

Based on designs by Joe Marc Freedman